How to be a...
MOTOCROSS CHAMPION

James Nixon

FRANKLIN WATTS
LONDON • SYDNEY

First published in 2015 by
Franklin Watts
338 Euston Road
London NW1 3BH

Franklin Watts Australia
Level 17/207 Kent Street
Sydney NSW 2000

© 2015 Franklin Watts

ISBN 978 1 4451 3629 5
Library eBook ISBN 978 1 4451 3631 8

Dewey classification number: 796

In preparation of this book, all due care has been exercised with regard to the advice, activities and techniques depicted. The publishers regret that they can accept no liability for any loss or injury sustained. When learning a new activity, it is important to get expert tuition and to follow a manufacturer's instructions.

A CIP catalogue record for this publication is available from the British Library.

Planning and production by Discovery Books Limited
Managing Editor: Paul Humphrey
Editor: James Nixon
Design: sprout.uk.com
Picture research: James Nixon

Printed in China

Franklin Watts is a division of Hachette Children's Books, an Hachette UK Company.
www.hachette.co.uk

Photo acknowledgements: Cover image (Shutterstock: mobill 11)
Alamy: pp. 7 top (Radharc Images), 12 (Steve Boyle/NewSport/ZUMAPRESS.com), 13 bottom (CTK/Alamy Live News), 15 top (Cesar Soares), 17 top (Action Plus Sports Images), 17 bottom (ZUMA Press, Inc), 19 top (Mark Draisey), 19 bottom (Stephen Bardens), 22 (EPA/OLIVIER HOSLET), 23 top (EPA/JAN WOITAS), 23 bottom (dpa picture alliance), 25 top (WENN Ltd), 25 bottom (Action Plus Sports Images), 26 (Erich Schlegel/NewSport/ZUMAPRESS.com), 27 top (Tribune Content Agency LLC), 27 bottom (Erich Schlegel/NewSport/ZUMAPRESS.com), 28 bottom (David Cattanach). Alpinestars: p. 9 top and middle. Kawasaki Motors: p. 6. Shutterstock: pp. 4 (Gines Romero), 5 top (sainthorant daniel), 7 bottom (Warren Price Photography), 8 (Pedro Monteiro), 9 bottom (sippakorn), 10 top (Tarczas), 10 bottom (PhotoStock10), 11 top (Keith Robinson), 11 bottom (Helga Esteb), 13 top (sippakorn), 14 (Marco Govel), 15 bottom (JASPERIMAGE), 16 (sippakorn), 18 (Juanan Barros Moreno), 20 (sippakorn), 21 top (sippakorn), 21 bottom (B Stefanov), 24 (Diego Barbieri), 28 top (Dmitry Kalinovsky), 29 top (sippakorn), 29 bottom (Warren Price Photography). Wikimedia: p. 5 bottom (Mark/Flickr).

Every attempt has been made to clear copyright. Should there be any inadvertent omission please apply to the publisher for rectification.

CONTENTS

All words in **bold** can be found in the glossary on page 31

WHAT IS MOTOCROSS?

Welcome to the high flying, fast and thrilling world of motocross (MX). In this incredible sport, up to 40 riders on special motorbikes race against each other on dirt tracks full of jumps and bumps.

IN IT TO WIN IT

The rules are simple. The rider who gets around the course first is the winner. A motocross track is about 1,500 to 2,000 metres long. As well as huge jumps, the tracks include fast, bumpy sections and tight corners. The battle for first place is fierce. Riders need strength, balance, quick **reflexes** and a whole lot of determination to come out on top.

A LITTLE BIT OF HISTORY

The first known motocross race took place in Surrey in England in 1924. Back then it was called scrambling. The bikes weren't very different to the ones found on the street. The courses didn't have many jumps because the bikes were not very strong. As motocross bike technology improved, so did the riders' skills and the sport's popularity grew. In 1966, motocross was introduced to the USA when an exhibition event was held in California. Motocross soon became a worldwide sport.

A motocross rider flies over the finish line to take the chequered flag and win the race.

Motocross races are fast, furious and enormous fun.

TOP DOG

A TASTE OF THE ACTION

The best thing about motocross is that anyone of any age or skill can ride an MX bike. If you love the idea of hitting the track, search the Internet for your local course and give it a shot. There are many places where you can hire a bike and gear and be coached in the basic skills. This will help you see if you enjoy riding motocross or not.

Twenty-eight-year-old Tony Cairoli (right) from Italy has already become one of the all-time greats of motocross. In 2009 he entered the World Championship in the MX1 engine class (the top class) for the first time. He won in style, coming first in nine races during the season. Cairoli has continued to dominate, winning every MX1 World Championship since. The question is, when will his winning streak end?

THE BIKE

Modern motocross bikes are highly specialised racing machines. They have ultra-tough **suspension** and powerful brakes. The bikes don't have huge top speeds, but they do have eye-watering acceleration.

Clutch lever – Pull this in while you are changing up a gear or when you are stopping.

Telescopic fork – Up to 33 centimetres of suspension at the front easily soaks up the bumps and jumps.

Throttle – Twist the grip backwards to speed up.

Sprocket and chain – transfers power to the rear wheel

Exhaust pipe – shaped to remove waste gases and increase the engine's power

Front brake lever

Rear brake pedal – (the gear shifter/pedal is on the opposite side)

Footpeg

Swing arm – **pivots** up and down as the wheel hits the bumps

Engine – Most bikes use **four-stroke** engines, which are less noisy and smoky than the **two-stroke** engines that used to be popular. The MX1 racing class is for 250cc two-strokes or 450cc four-strokes. The MX2 class is for smaller engines – 125cc two-strokes or 250cc four-strokes.

Tyres – With their chunky **tread** the tyres can grip the loose dirt in any conditions.

Disc brakes – When you brake, pads grip on to these discs for fast braking. The front brake does most of the work to slow the bike down.

BUYING A BIKE

Buying a second-hand bike is best for a beginner. Check your local newspaper and motocross shops for adverts and you should find plenty of cheap bikes for sale. It's important to check the bike is in good condition. Look for parts that might be worn, such as the sprockets and brakes, and push down on the fork to check the suspension is working smoothly.

It is a good idea to start with a smaller engine size, as you will be safer. Check that the bike works for you. You should be able to reach the bars and all the levers comfortably while sitting or standing.

AIR BOX COVER
No-Toil
FREE
Toil

Protect your bike during a wash with air box and exhaust covers.

BIKE CARE

Getting your bike muddy is a lot more fun than washing it off, but this needs to be done as soon as possible after a race. Before you hose down the worst of the dirt, you need to buy special covers for your exhaust and air box **filter** to stop the water getting in. The dirt that is left then needs to be scrubbed off with soapy water using a sponge and brush. Rinse the suds off and apply bike **lube** to your chain to stop it rusting.

RECORD BREAKERS

In 2002, Ricky Carmichael from Florida, USA, rode the perfect American Motorcyclist Association (AMA) Motocross Championship season, winning all 24 races! Two years later he amazingly did it again. The record is literally unbeatable. However, it was equalled by fellow Florida rider, James 'Bubba' Stewart (right) in 2008 (see page 26).

GEAR GUIDE

Motocross is a high-speed sport and accidents happen. The best way to lower the risk of being hurt is to wear the correct safety kit.

When you take your goggles to a race, keep them in a plastic bag so that they don't get dirty.

HELMET

A helmet is the most important piece of protection you can buy. The safest option is to buy a brand new full-face helmet. It should fit snugly on your head so it doesn't bounce about, but it should not crush your head either. Buckle the strap tightly below your chin so the helmet can't fly off during a crash.

GOGGLES

Eye injuries can be serious so always wear goggles. Make sure you buy a pair that fits inside your helmet. Before you race, you can apply thin films of clear plastic to the goggles called tear-offs. If mud lands on your goggles you can tear the film off and regain your vision.

GLOVES

Gloves should fit snugly so that you have a good feel for the controls. However, check that they are not too tight around the webbing of your fingers. Race gloves have extra padding in the palms to protect you in a fall.

BODY ARMOUR

Chest and back protectors worn under a race jersey shield your upper body in crashes. They also take the sting out of any flying dirt or stones thrown up from tyres. A kidney belt supports the lower back and protects some of your vital **organs**.

To protect your knees, you have two choices. You can use the knee and shin cups that come with most race trousers, or knee pads or braces. If you plan on buying braces make sure they fit under your clothes. Elbow pads are also a good idea for beginners.

STAYING SAFE

Do not be fooled. Even if you wear armour from head to toe, you can still get hurt. Always ride within your limits. If you feel you are losing control, reduce your speed and move on to a smoother piece of the course. Otherwise you are a danger to other riders as well as yourself. When practising, never ride alone, because if you crash there will be no one to help.

BOOTS

A proper pair of motocross boots is vital. Feet and ankles take a lot of knocks so the boots are tough with hard plastic protectors. Try out as many different pairs as you can. They should hold your ankles snugly, but they shouldn't be so stiff that you find it hard to use the pedals.

Crashes are common in motocross, so do everything you can to stay safe.

STARTING OUT

Before you start entering races you will need lots of practice. If you are new to motocross, visit your local track early in the morning. The course will be much smoother and you can concentrate on your skills rather than battling the track.

PRACTICE MAKES PERFECT

When you practise, concentrate on using the different controls so that you can learn their limits. Motocross races are often won and lost in the corners. A good way to practise cornering is to find an area where you can do circles or figure-of-eights. Practise obstacles such as jumps and **ruts** until you are completely confident. A good tip is to ride close to other riders so that it feels like a true race.

Beginners should spend a lot of time practising their cornering skills.

You need to practise the correct body position until it becomes natural.

BODY POSITION

The 'attack' position is a crucial technique. Whether you are sitting or standing, your weight should be centred over the seat with both feet on the **footpegs**. Look ahead down the track, keeping your head above the handlebars. Raise your elbows high so that your body can cope with a blast of speed. Your knees should be slightly bent, even while standing. This acts as extra suspension. Squeeze the seat with your knees so that you feel like a part of the bike.

Motocross riders are constantly adjusting their body as the speed and **terrain** changes. Don't be a statue on the bike. Keep your upper body relaxed so that you can move about to stay balanced.

ON THE MOVE

The throttle is controlled by twisting the grip with your right hand. Start in the over-grip position with your knuckles pointed to the ground. This makes it easier for you to open the throttle the whole way. Don't apply too much throttle too quickly, because your rear wheel will just spin. Try to select the right gear for the track ahead. It becomes easy with practice.

Always have one or two fingers covering the clutch lever. Clutch control can help you accelerate. As you accelerate hard, pull the clutch a little at the same time to help you build up power quicker. If you are struggling in too high a gear, you can pull the clutch in slightly to get the engine up to speed.

Use one or two fingers on the clutch, and keep them there at all times.

RECORD BREAKERS

Ashley Fiolek (left) from the USA was born with impaired hearing in 1990. This hasn't stopped her becoming a motocross superstar. Fiolek started racing at the age of 7. In 2008, aged 18, she became the youngest winner of the Women's AMA Motocross Championship ever. By 2012 she had won another three titles.

BRAKING AND CORNERING

The art of good braking and cornering is again down to body position. The brakes can be used for more than slowing down. Tapping the rear brake can keep the bike in a straight line or make the rear wheel stay down.

SLOWING DOWN

When you brake, move your weight back towards the rear of the seat to balance the bike. Try to do most of your braking in a straight line before you start turning. Most of the time both brakes should be used together. Pull the levers smoothly and gradually. If you pull too hard, the front wheel will lock up and you will start to skid.

When racing downhill you need to brake much earlier. Plan your braking carefully. If you brake hard on a bump you could be thrown over the handlebars. Try to brake before and after bumps and let the suspension do the work over bumpy ground. Instead choose a spot to brake which offers the most grip. Try to avoid braking in sand or mud.

Keeping your weight back when you brake keeps the back end of the bike on the ground.

MAKING TURNS

On a flat turn, you need to lower your **centre of gravity**. This means sitting down and sliding forward to the front of the seat. Stick out your inside leg as you come off the brakes and put pressure on the outside footpeg with your outside elbow raised. In case you need to **dab** the inside foot, keep your toes pointed upwards.

In motocross you should always be braking or accelerating. At most corners, move from hard braking to lighter and lighter braking until you need to accelerate out of the corner. Pick one gear for the corner and stick with it.

Try to make wide turns so you can keep your speed up. Look for any banked corners and ruts that you could use to help you turn harder and faster. These give you more **traction**, but avoid deep ruts that you could get stuck in.

Raise your outside elbow above the handlebar when you corner.

BRAKE SLIDE

If you need to change direction sharply, you can pull off a brake slide. To do this, stand on the rear brake to lock the back wheel up as you turn the bike to face the right way.

TOP DOG

Jeffrey Herlings (left) from the Netherlands has gradually risen through the ranks to become a double World Champion in the MX2 class. In 2004 Herlings was Dutch Champion in the 65cc engine class. By 2008 he was European and World Champion in the 85cc class. He stepped up yet again to MX2 in 2009. After finishing runner-up in the 2011 World Championship, Herlings' patience was finally rewarded, winning the MX2 world title the next two seasons.

JUMPING

Jumping is one of the most important parts of motocross and, for many, the most fun. To be successful, you must master the air as well as the ground, so learn the techniques carefully.

START SMALL

When learning to jump, start with small, single jumps. Don't try larger jumps, **tabletops**, doubles and triples until you are 100 per cent confident.

The key to controlling a jump is the take-off. Look before you leap; you should always plan where you want to take off and land. As you approach the jump, keep your weight centred in the 'attack' position. As you leave the ramp, ease off the throttle and lean back slightly. The most common mistake is to tense up at this point – stay relaxed.

AIR TO LAND

Be ready to lean slightly in mid-air to help keep the bike level. You can pull the clutch in and touch the rear brake to lower the front wheel. Applying the throttle can lower the rear wheel.

On fast jumps or in rough ground, it may help to land the rear wheel slightly before the front. As you land, use a little throttle and bend your knees and elbows to soften the landing.

The controls of a motocross bike are just as important when you are in mid-air.

Riders need lots of speed to clear a double jump.

TABLETOPS AND DOUBLES

On a tabletop jump you need to clear the flat top and land on the **downslope**. It's all about speed and timing. If you get it right and think you will land on the downslope, push forward on the handlebars to lower the front of the bike. Once the bike is level with the angle of the slope, shift your weight back before you land.

Doubles are for the experts only. These are two jumps close together that need to be cleared at the same time. If you underjump and don't make it to the other side, you can crash badly.

DROP-OFFS

Drop-offs are tough obstacles with hard landings. To handle a sudden drop, shift your weight back and extend your legs as you drop. Now you can collapse your arms and legs when you land to soak up the shock.

RECORD BREAKERS

In 2012, a 19-year-old from Washington, USA, landed the biggest ever motocross jump in history. Alex Harvill soared 130 metres, smashing the previous record of 119 metres held by famous Australian daredevil Robbie Maddison. Harvill thinks he can go well past 150 metres in the future but is happy to let his record stand for a while!

On jumps or drops you should usually be standing the whole time.

RUTS AND WHOOPS

Ruts and whoops are two other types of obstacles that motocross riders must learn to master. Ruts are deep channels created by the bike's tyres. Whoops are bumpy sections of track.

STUCK IN A RUT

Once your wheels drop into the groove of a rut, there is little you can do to change direction. This means you need to look and plan ahead, and only ride into ruts that take you on a good line. The ruts on a course are forever changing. The fastest rut on one lap may make your life a misery the next lap. For example, a rut can get so deep that it slows the bike down.

IN THE GROOVE

Try to enter a rut as straight as possible with both wheels, so that you can flow with the groove. Keep your front wheel in the centre of the rut and your toes pointed upwards so that they don't catch the rut wall. You need to be riding smoothly. Jerky movements or a pull on the brake can cause you to lose control and balance.

You may need to shift your body to keep the bike in the centre of a rut.

WHOOP WHOOP

Whoops are some of the toughest tests of a rider's skill. You need to pick the smoothest and straightest line possible through the whoops so that the suspension can work properly. Stand up on the footpegs so that you can absorb the bumps with your knees and are ready to shift your weight about.

Aim to land on top of the whoops, rather than in the troughs. As you skim over shallow bumps, shift your weight towards the back of the seat and keep the front wheel up. Too much weight on the front could cause you to stab into a whoop and send you over the bars. It helps to pick a gear that will give you a quick burst of speed when needed.

Whoops can be too far apart to skim, but close enough to double jump. To get extra lift on your jump, bend your knees and push the bike down on the face of the ramp. As you take off, the suspension will rebound, giving you that extra boost of height.

The pros can skim over whoops and make them look easy.

TOP DOG

American Ricky Carmichael (left) has been given the nickname 'The GOAT', standing for Greatest of All Time. He was unbeatable for a decade. Between 1997 and 1999 he won every MX2 AMA Championship. From 2000 he won the MX1 AMA Championship seven years running! At the age of 27 Carmichael retired from motocross to become a stock car racer.

RACE DAY

If you feel you are ready to start racing, find a local race meeting in your area. Races are divided by ages and engine sizes. Even the experts get nervous on race day. Don't worry about it – it's part of racing.

BE PREPARED

Nothing is worse for racing than showing up late. Try to organise everything you need to bring to the track the night before and arrive early. By not feeling rushed you can focus on your race much better. The first thing you must do is pay your race fee – check in advance how much it will cost. Then you need to head to the registration area where you will be given your race number.

On race day, watch the other races for some tips on how best to ride the track.

TRACK WALK

Always walk around the track before you race. This gives you a slow-motion view of what you will be flying over. You can learn the layout, start planning the ruts and jumps you want to use and work out which parts of the track you want to avoid.

Use your practice session to warm up and test out different lines. It's a good idea to watch as much of the other riders as possible to see how they are tackling different obstacles.

A yellow flag means caution. It is used to tell the racers to drive slowly if there is a crash on the course.

RACE RULES

A race meeting takes the riders through the rules of the event. It pays to listen because the rules will be different at each track. There are normally qualifying races called **motos**. If you do well in these you qualify for the final, which decides the overall winner. The top qualifiers also get to choose their **starting gate** positions for the final.

FLAGS

At most tracks a yellow flag is waved if there is a problem on the track, such as a crash. Passing is not allowed during a yellow flag, and you should be aware and in control of your bike. A red flag indicates a more serious crash. Riders must slow to 5 mph (8 kph) and return to the starting gate. A blue flag tells you to pull over because you are about to be **lapped**. The white flag shows you that there is just one lap left to go.

RECORD BREAKERS

Stefan Everts (below) from Belgium is the most successful World Championship rider of all time. He won a record ten world titles in various classes, including a record six in the premier MX1 class. The five-time Belgian Sportsman of the Year retired in 2006. Everts was famous for his smooth style and the amount of time he stayed standing on the bike, even in tight corners.

BATTLING FOR POSITION

The start is the most important part of the race. If you grab an early lead you don't have to worry about mud, dust and traffic slowing you down. Start badly and you will have to fight your way past a lot of other riders to win.

THE HOLESHOT

Taking the lead at the first corner is called getting the **holeshot**. Have a plan of the line you want to aim for at the first corner. At the starting gate, hold your balance by keeping both feet on the ground in front of the footpegs. Sit as far forward on the bike as you can with your head over the handlebars. Now open the throttle about halfway and keep your eyes firmly on the gate as you wait for it to drop.

OUT OF THE GATE

For a quick getaway, you need to find the point where the clutch is pulled in just enough to keep the bike from moving. When the gate drops, let the clutch out and turn to full power quickly, but smoothly. Get both feet on the pegs as soon as possible so that you are ready to shift up a gear.

The last thing you want is wheelspin or you will be left behind. To avoid wheelspin, don't rev the engine too much or let go of the clutch too quickly. The rear wheel will have better grip if you brush off any loose dirt at your gate before the start.

Riders power away from the starting gate.

Battling for position is one of the most thrilling parts of motocross.

OVERTAKING

The best way to pass another rider is to use a different line from them. Then if they make a mistake, you can slip by fairly easily. Overtaking at corners is a common tactic. You can pass a rider on the inside of a turn and then drift out on to their line in front of them, so that they have to let go of the throttle. This is called block passing. If a rider is scared of being block passed they may ride on the inside of the corner, meaning you can fly by on the outside.

The best riders can take advantage of their skills and make passes on obstacles. Whoops are a good place to pass if you can find a faster line.

UNDER PRESSURE

Even if you can't overtake, it's a good idea to ride close to your rival in front, to show them that you are just behind. This can make them nervous and force them into making a mistake, leaving you an easy chance to pass. You can even grab the clutch and rev your engine to scare them! Don't wait too long before you make your move or other riders will catch up with you.

You can pass a rider on the whoops if they make a mistake.

THE BIG EVENTS

The Motocross World Championship and the AMA Motocross Championship are the two biggest motocross series in the world. These are the events that the top pros train for years to take part in.

A rider battles the sand at the World Championship track in Lommel, Belgium.

TOP OF THE WORLD

The first Motocross World Championship took place in 1957. Today, the tournament is held over 18 rounds, staged at tracks across the world. Most rounds take place in Europe, but there are also races held in Asia, Australia, Africa and South America. At every round there are two races to decide the overall winner. Each race lasts for 35 minutes, plus a final two laps.

DIG DEEP

The World Championship track in Lommel, Belgium, is one of the most famous and feared in the world. The riders literally have to dig deep as their bikes carve through the bottomless sand. Sand races are tough on your bike and your body. You need to be fit both mentally and physically.

THE AMA

The American Motorcyclist Association (AMA) Motocross Championship is held over 12 rounds at 12 different tracks across the United States. The series began in 1972. Today it attracts riders from all over the world. In 2014, the title was won by German starlet Ken Roczen who was just 20 years old.

MOTOCROSS DES NATIONS

The Motocross des Nations has been called the 'Olympics of Motocross'. It is held every year at a different location. Each nation has a team of three riders. The points scored by the three riders are added together to find the winning country. The USA have had some incredible winning streaks, taking the title every year between 1981–1993, and 2005–2011.

Racers from 41 nations took part in the 2013 Motocross des Nations in Teutschenthal, Germany.

Ken Roczen turned pro in 2009 at the age of 14, but he was not allowed to race in the World Championships until he turned 15. Roczen didn't take long to make an impact. At 15 years and 53 days old he became the youngest person to ever win a round of the World Championship when he came first at his home event in Germany in the MX2 class. A year later he became MX2 World Champion.

Ken Roczen jumps over a hill during the Motocross des Nations.

SUPERCROSS

Supercross is a spectacular form of indoor motocross. The tracks are smaller, with shorter straights and tighter turns. The jumps are crazier and steeper. The riders seem to spend as much time in the air as they do on the track!

THE CROWDS

Supercross is a big sport in the USA. To build the tracks, enormous amounts of soil are transported into huge sports stadiums. Fans pack the stadiums to watch their heroes in action. They can get a stunning birds-eye view of the riders as they fly over the jumps, whoops and banked corners on the course.

TOP DOG

Ryan Villopoto is the man to beat in supercross right now. The 26-year-old, born in Fortuna, California, has won the AMA Supercross Championship for the last four years. In 2014 he finished on 368 points, 64 points clear of his nearest rival Ryan Dungey. In 2011 and 2013, Villopoto also won the AMA Motocross Championship in the MX1 class. Villopoto is an expert at riding when the track conditions are tough and becomes even harder to beat.

Supercross is an exciting and challenging form of motocross.

THE CHAMPIONSHIP

The AMA Supercross Championship is held over 17 rounds in stadiums all over North America. The races are short (up to 20 laps) and action-packed. Riders have to battle hard to overtake and big crashes sometimes happen. The winner of a round pockets 25 Championship points. The rider with the most points at the end of the season wins the Championship.

One of the AMA Supercross Championship rounds is held at the famous Daytona International Speedway racetrack. The supercross track is built on an island between the **pit lane** and the circuit.

American Jeremy McGrath (below) earned the title 'King of Supercross' in the 1990s. He won seven AMA Supercross Championships between 1993 and 2000 and 72 races in total, achieving a record that is yet to be beaten. McGrath would wow the crowds by pulling off tricks during his jumps in races.

Ryan Villopoto wins a round of the AMA Supercross Championship at the Daytona International Speedway in Florida.

STORY OF A CHAMPION

JAMES 'BUBBA' STEWART

James 'Bubba' Stewart is famous for being the first African-American to reach the top of a major motorsport. Superstar Stewart is a genius on two wheels. The speed and the lines he chooses as he cruises around the track seem unreal at times. Here is the story of how he made it to the top.

Like many racers, Stewart competes in motocross and supercross and has had huge success in both.

EARLY STARTER

Born in Bartow, Florida, in 1985, Stewart was already entering motocross races at the age of 4! His dad loved motorcycles so much that he had taught Stewart to ride a dirt bike when he was just 3 years old. Amazingly Stewart won the first of his Amateur National titles aged 6. In 1997 Stewart's dad bought 16 **hectares** of land so that he could build a practice track in the back garden!

TURNING PRO

In 2002, in his first season as a pro, Stewart became the youngest person ever to win the MX2 AMA Motocross Championship and was named AMA **Rookie** of the Year. In the April 2003 issue of *Teen People* magazine he was named one of the '20 Teens Who Will Change the World'. In 2004 he won the Eastern Division of the MX2 Supercross Championship and the outdoor national title again.

James Stewart had little trouble stepping up to the top level of motocross racing.

A BIGGER BIKE

Stewart had proven himself and it was now time to make the step up to the top division – the MX1 class with 450cc engines. Like many riders, Stewart found handling the bigger bikes tough and spent a lot of time hitting the dirt. However, he soon got the hang of it, winning his first supercross race at the Texas Stadium in 2005. In 2007 he won his first AMA Supercross Championship.

BOUNCING BACK

Part of being a motocross rider is picking up bad injuries. The test for a rider is how they bounce back. Stewart did this in awesome fashion. After missing the 2008 supercross season with a knee injury, Stewart went on to race the perfect outdoor Motocross Championship later that year, winning 24 out of the 24 races!

In 2009 Stewart and his close rival, Australian Chad Reed, were involved in one of the toughest Supercross Championships ever. Stewart eventually won the last race in Las Vegas to take the title by just four points. He continues to challenge for titles and is fast catching Jeremy McGrath's (see page 25) record of 72 supercross race wins.

Stewart on his way to winning the 2009 AMA Supercross Championship.

GAINING AN EDGE

To be a motocross star you need more than just talent. Motocross is one of the hardest sports you'll ever try. You need to be in top shape physically and have lots of dedication.

FITNESS

The top motocross racers are as fast at the end of a race as they are at the beginning. That's because they have trained hard and have bucket-loads of stamina. Running, swimming and cycling are all good activities if you need to improve your general level of fitness.

Motocross is punishing on lots of your muscles, especially your lower back, thighs, shoulders and neck. Make sure you do plenty of exercises that strengthen these areas. Mountain biking is a useful training activity because it is fun and uses many of the same muscle groups.

STRETCH

Stretching before a race is the best preparation for the punishment your body is about to be put through. Do simple stretches for your arms, legs and back, such as touching your toes. It's important to get the blood flowing before you race so swing your arms and jog on the spot. It can even help to break a sweat in your warm-up.

Motocross racers need to train hard to reach the very top.

If you don't drink enough on race day you won't be able to perform.

Having a race plan at the starting gate will help you focus and give you a better chance of winning.

DIET

As with any tough activity, your body needs fuel to perform properly. A good diet will help you race better. Cut out as much sugary and junk food from your diet as you can and eat plenty of **carbohydrates**, such as pasta, in the days leading up to the race. On race day, keep it simple. The last thing you want is a full stomach. Cereal for breakfast and an energy-packed peanut butter sandwich is a good choice. Also make sure you drink enough to keep you going throughout the race.

POWER OF THE MIND

The best racers are determined and highly focused on improving their riding skills. They learn how to tinker with their bike **set-up** to get the best out of their machine. They form strategies of how they are going to win a race. They work hard, give their all and never give up. Just remember, there is a lot more to racing than powering the throttle.

RECORD BREAKERS

Jessica Patterson (below) is one of the most successful riders in the history of women's motocross. Between 2000 and 2013 she won a record seven AMA Championships. Her aggressive riding style and endless hours of practice and training have helped her to dominate the competition.

29

FIND OUT MORE

BOOKS

Motocross Greats,
Lori Polydoros, (Capstone Press 2011)

**Motocross Skills: How to Be an Ace
Motocross Rider**,
Anthony Sutton, (A & C Black Publishers 2012)

**Pro Motocross and Off-road Riding
Techniques**,
Donnie Bales, (Motorbooks International 2004)

To the Limit: Motocross,
Gary Freeman, (PowerKids Press 2012)

WEBSITES

www.wikihow.com/Category:Dirt-Bikes
A series of 'How to…' guides for motocross riders

**http://stage.theadrenalist.com/extreme/
motocross-starter-guide**
Videos and advice to help you improve your
motocross racing skills

**www.superfreestylemotocross.com/
blog/10-tips-to-improve-dirt-bike-
motocross-riding-technique**
Ten useful tips to improve your riding technique

**http://victory-sports.com/archives/
Beginner%20race%20info.htm**
A beginner's guide for motocross riders who
want to start racing

**http://motocross.transworld.net/category/
riding-tips**
An in-depth website with race news and
videos to help you ride and look after your dirt
bike better

www.dirtbikerider.com/tracks
Find a motocross track near you

Website disclaimer: Note to parents and teachers: Every
effort has been made by the Publishers to ensure that
these websites are suitable for children, that they are of
the highest educational value, and that they contain no
inappropriate or offensive material. However, because of
the nature of the Internet, it is impossible to guarantee
that the contents of these sites will not be altered. We
strongly advise that Internet access is supervised by a
responsible adult.

GLOSSARY

carbohydrates a group of foods that can be broken down to release energy in the body

centre of gravity the imaginary point in a body where the total weight of the body is concentrated

dab touch the ground with a foot

downslope a downward slope on a motocross track

filter a device that removes unwanted particles when a liquid or gas is passed through it

footpegs the metal platforms on a motorbike where the rider places their feet

four-stroke an engine that fires after two up-and-down movements (four strokes) of the piston

hectare a unit of measure equal to 10,000 square metres

holeshot the lead position at the first corner

lapped overtaken so that you are over one lap behind the rider who has just passed you

lube a substance for greasing (lubricating) a part of a machine

moto a race in which riders attempt to place high enough in order to qualify for the final

organ a part of the body that performs a vital function, such as the heart or kidney

pit lane the piece of track that motor racing drivers drive down to make repairs or refuel

pivot turn on a fixed central point

reflexes responses by parts of the body

rookie a new member of a sports team

rut a groove in the track created by the wheels of motorbikes

set-up the way your vehicle is tuned (adjusted) for a race

starting gate a raised barrier at the start of a motocross race

suspension the system of springs and shock absorbers on a vehicle

tabletop a jump with a flat section of dirt filled in between a take-off and landing ramp

terrain the features of a piece of land

traction the grip of a tyre on a road or track

tread the part of a tyre that grips the road or track

two-stroke an engine that fires after one up-and-down movement (two strokes) of the piston

INDEX